Thad DeVassie

SPLENDID IRRATIONALITIES

Prose Poems

SurVision Books

First published in 2021 by
SurVision Books
Dublin, Ireland
Reggio di Calabria, Italy
www.survisionmagazine.com

Copyright © Thad DeVassie, 2021

Cover image: "It Is Finished" by James Kaniaris
© James Kaniaris, 2021

ISBN: 978-1-912963-25-6

This book is in copyright. No part of this publication may be reproduced, stored in a retrieval system, or transmitted in any form or by any means without the prior permission in writing from the publisher.

Acknowledgments

Grateful acknowledgment is made to the editors of the following, in which some of these poems, or versions of them, originally appeared:

Back Patio Press: "The Dawn of Spectator Sports"

Fiction Kitchen Berlin: "The Scientist and the Magician"

Juked: "Zen and the Art of Evel Knievel"

Spelk: "All the Covers"

Sublunary Review: "House of Plates, 1872"

Ucity Review: "The Procrastinator's Story"

Unbroken: "Everything is Random"

Notes

"Ronco Poetry Infomercial" acknowledges entities formed, patented and trademarked by Ron Popeil including Ronco Corporation, GLH-9 (Great Looking Hair Formula #9) Hair in a Can Spray, and Chop-o-Matic/Veg-o-Matic products.

"Things That Squawk" references elements from the title poem to the collection *The Reason Why the Closet-Man Is Never Sad* by Russell Edson (Wesleyan University Press, 1977), and the short story "The Book" from *Stories for Nighttime and Some for the Day* by Ben Loory (Penguin Books, 2011).

The title "Zen and the Art of Evel Knievel" and references therein are modified after the book, *Zen and the Art of Motorcycle Maintenance* by Robert Pirsig (William Morrow and Company, 1974). "House of Plates, 1872" references the photography of Mathew Brady, which are in the public domain.

The Sneeze^{TM} is for literary effect only. It is not a registered trademark.

Contents

Everything Is Random	5
Café Sputnik	6
Some Considerations Before Dropping It	7
The Scientist and the Magician	8
Ghost Bus	10
The Old Dogs	11
Space Lust	12
Ronco Poetry Infomercial	13
Sunsets and Folklore from the North Country	14
Novocaine	15
All the Covers	16
Theme Song for a Nondescript Gentleman	18
The Dawn of Spectator Sports	21
The Procrastinator's Story	22
Physical Comedy	23
The Sneeze ™	24
Zen and the Art of Evel Knievel	26
Small Talk with the Dead	27
House of Plates, 1872	28
Near Death Experience	29
Things That Squawk	30

Everything Is Random

When a thief pried his way into our home with the intent to pillage and inflict harm, I didn't flinch. Instead, I said, *follow me,* and we walked out the back door, avoiding the neighbor's peering eyes and resulting gossip, then made our way a half-dozen blocks to the corner mini-mart. With the exception of our awkward dance projected on a grainy, closed-circuit security monitor, we moved undetected as we passed the Slushie machine and overcooked roller food, until we could spot bounties of promise: A deck of playing cards. Lock de-icer and Duralogs. Sudoku and disposable razors. Beef jerky and more beef jerky. The stuff of impulse and biding one's time, of uncommon necessity and banal utility in the dark hours damn near close to this one. How it all found its way into four prized aisles of a near-vacant mini-mart awash in fluorescent lighting remains a distant supply chain secret, as perplexing as the novice cat burglar who, without his stocking cap and nude panty hose screening his face, is just another domesticated animal looking to make it through the day.

Café Sputnik

Vlad and I had been at it for more than an hour, a feisty give and take of opinion and hyperbole, our debate rising above the diner's hum of conversation and clanking dishware by a novice busser. He was rambling and using ridiculous analogies, something about a one-armed paper hanger in a three-legged sack race, when I made the assertion: *Technically speaking, you cannot be a cosmonaut, Vlad. You're from Georgia. The U.S. state. Not the former Soviet Union. It's astronaut or bust.* I questioned my curtness as we sat in uncomfortable silence, reminiscent of a Cold War stalemate.

Then I noticed how my dinner companion kept finger-tracing a coffee stain on his paper placemat resembling Gorbachev's birthmark. We heard an old woman begging for rubles on the stoop outside the diner, watching every papery proceed go into her babushka hat. A patron at an adjacent table ordered littleneck clams and received a piping hot bowl with a tiny sickle and hammer to pry open the shells. The novice busboy busied himself with decaf refills from a fresh pot, replacing soiled placemats from a stack crisp and bright as white-hot constellations. He winked at Vlad. His nametag read Cosmo. As we stepped outside the diner my arm detached from my body, slipped through my shirt and coat sleeves, and fell to the ground with the clank of a dead warhead, smashing my big toe. Vlad smiled sheepishly after he realized we weren't in eminent danger. He leaned in to give me support as I hopped like a child on one leg. When we left the diner, I put the unarmed warhead on the stoop should someone want to sell it for scrap. The begging woman was long gone, but the moon outside was remarkably low and full and almost within reach. I questioned everything I assumed was true as we watched satellites streaking across the night sky.

Some Considerations Before Dropping It

The f-bomb exists on a sliding scale between dynamite and kryptonite – ill-timed and in the wrong hands with the wrong tone or the wrong context, it might detonate, obliterate what could've been a knockout narrative had different diction prevailed.

Take precaution:

> Consider translating the *uck* into a Morse-like coding of asterisks and symbols next to that flagpole of an F;
>
> Postulate on the speculative underline as a burial mine for filling in what the reader knows is missing;
>
> See if you can't shirk the fact that a two-letter abbreviated nod to vulgarity including a beloved *mother* seems ill-conceived; then
>
> Pause on this whole pursuit of profanity for profanity's sake, expletives as interchangeable nouns, adjectives, adverbs, verbs – sometimes in the same blankety-blank line.

Then note how threading well-scrubbed language falls short of your pungent anger, your righteous indignation. It's times like these that one feels like an unseen extra in *GoodFellas,* minding one's own business at Morrie's Wig Shop just before De Niro unleashes a barrage of mother-bleeping sentiments and New York ball-busting, throwing sacrilege and haymakers in your direction to the point where you need some cover and an Al Pacino-enraged line from *Heat* that feels necessary if not retaliatory, absolving you from any wrongdoing and putting you back on even footing as you decide to drop it – *"don't waste my motherfucking time!"*

The Scientist and the Magician

Elena carries around a pill box dispenser in the shape of the periodic table of elements. Each tiny compartment contains a small but different pill. When we head out for dinner, she's discreet about her pill popping despite nothing being discreet about a woman in fine health carrying a pill box with 118 miniscule compartments. She takes them at random, for no particular reason that is obvious. She claims it is just her thing.

I've become comfortable with the stares, the prying eyes, these strange scientific shenanigans she plays for an audience that doesn't know her plot or endgame. Yet I don't ask Elena what lies under the plastic lid of Bismuth, a place I swear we visited last winter, or Dysprosium, which I also believe I spied advertised on TV with encouragement to ask my doctor if it's right for what ails me. She reminds me this is her happy hijinks, a dose of the off-kilter for an otherwise serious woman of science.

Tonight she's particularly aglow for a night on the town. She puts a sliver of something atop her tongue from one of the compartments with the letters He on it. She wraps herself in a vibrant assortment of shawls and scarves as we prepare for the evening.

You'll need a hat, she informs, tossing me a black, pop-open top hat. I retort: *That ridiculous hat? I'll look like a magician.* She pouts, waits, until I oblige.

We leave her flat and walk toward the town strip of taco trucks, dive bars and cantinas, her hand entwined with mine, until she starts pulling away as if some mysterious current has her, leaving behind a spindly end of her scarf, its opposite end tied to another scarf, and then another. Impossibly, Elena is now levitating, no, floating, and also unraveling, each scarf and shawl that comprised her outfit unwinding like thread from a spool with no end. Elena escapes a good fifty feet or so into the air and I fear she'll be nearly nude in no time except for her dazzling heels. A crowd begins to form and gawk skyward as I pull on colorful scarves as though it were one long tug-of-war rope connected to *Elena the Balloon* or *Elena the Kite Girl* who has become infinitely smaller from ground level, her scarves and shawls appearing more elaborate than the standard rainbow of handkerchiefs streaming from a magician's hat. As we perform this little atomic number, two to be precise, as in Elena and me, or Helium and her, this impromptu side show on 81st street is gaining wild applause as I'm piecing it together, screeching out some version of falsetto-Helium encouragement while simultaneously failing her, incapable of flipping the top hat from my head for tips in fear of losing my grip.

Ghost Bus

What do they know of death, the foot-tired and the weary with their parcels, their itineraries? Then like a dawning, an epiphany, they start inching away from curbsides, from shelter benches, becoming quick converts to pedestrianism, believing there is another way and politely waving to the reaper behind the wheel who won't stop until he reaches capacity.

The Old Dogs

The neighbor's dog Oscar is a crotchety old breed, a bit of a slow mover. Each morning he plods patiently across a property line he doesn't acknowledge, sniffing through the morning dew in search of a place to place his business.

I don't bother to bark.

And here comes the neighbor, equally old and crotchety, his hand outstretched and wrapped in plastic grocery sacks, prepared to perform a pet-owner's duty. How curious, this man with dung in hand, who celebrates Oscar's business then berates the neighborhood kids, imploring them to stay off his damn lawn.

Space Lust

Moonshot at 50

There was something hopeful, so highly enticing about the moon's mysteriousness, this burning desire to get acquainted. Oh, the lunar lunacy of it all.

Then we danced, kicked up some dust, and planted our flags in the name of space lust.

And like that, it was over.

Moon, it is your fullness that brings out the worst in us; your waxing, waning, and new disappearing act, all of it having lost that early allure now that Mars, adorned in hedonistic red, seduces rover to come on over while Venus, throwing some shade, awaits her eventual, orbital turn.

Ronco Poetry Infomercial

Ron is at it again, hawking new words of wisdom in the middle of the night, high on the cable dial. His smart set of applause-happy guests and cheery directors are in a lather over *Foot, Line & Meter* – the everyman's manifesto to poetry publishing success – which becomes truncated to FLM, a nod to his GLH-9 days.

"Be dazzled," proclaims Ron, "as you're about to be awash in a litany of lines from housewives, mechanics and undertakers, all of whom are writing with the moxie of Stevens, the eloquence of Cummings, the urgency of Plath..." his purported claims sewn together into a classic Popeilian sonnet. We are told how one fine miner-poet found himself accepted into *Pandora's Boxers* and *Appalachian Haiku Quarterly* in the same week. This is just the greasing of his o-Matic skids that has made the Jersey pitchman legendary.

Sandwiched between a *Golden Girls* episode and a Flex Seal pitch, I never saw the infomercial again. But Popeil, the master of interruption and intrigue, is ridiculously lyrical, recalled like a break-up song at the sight of an old lover, whether it is among a sea of balding men or down the dial at the sight of a televangelist's stage presence. Every time a canary comes to mind I am reminded of that miner, then the housewife. That's when I stop to pray for all the good people in *Pandora's Boxers*, hoping they're doing all they can to keep it filled with the good stuff.

Sunsets and Folklore from the North Country

There's something about the way a blood-orange sun gets pulled down each night with such preciseness, lassoed by Paul Bunyan, steadily dragged out of sight so darkness can have its moment, only to be flung from his rope like a slingshot toward the other side of the planet.

He being a lumbering, gigantic-sized version of what it means to be industrious, something akin to King Kong or Godzilla emerging from thick brush or a few miles off a crowded beach, towering over cities, always mindful that one misstep in his steel-toed boots wipes out a small hamlet.

It's enough to make you wonder if he saw the end of his logging career on the horizon and chose something more renewable, if he carries on solo or if some monstrous Babe joins him, if not for the companionship on those long global walks, perhaps to cast a broad and necessary shadow and, at the least, to apply sunscreen now and then on his blistering neck.

Novocaine

For Charles Simic

She found what he had left behind – all those remnants from his lunch hour, which he assumed would happen with her skillful probing. He sat chaired, defenseless, unable to speak; her latex-covered fingers and metallic hooks working his stretched mouth like an angler to the prized fish.

He fed her elaborate lies of hygiene when in truth he ceased the rinse, abandoned the floss in exchange for longer sittings where her beaming blue eyes focused on him, and vice versa, anticipating the snap of the rubber glove after her finger took a slow cruise along his bloodied gum line.

This mistaken flirtation, his faux courtship capsized when he felt that prick of her drill driving into his soft, decaying enamel, it being a terrible accompaniment to her whispered declaration to trust her, and that he wouldn't feel a thing.

All the Covers

A cover is both the teaser, a salacious or magnetic hook, and fierce protector of contents. It is judged despite friendly advice you've long been receiving.

A cover up is to hide all that is unflattering. It is a caretaker's sweet gesture reserved for children, and sleeping lovers before they eventually leave.

Cover crops do what's necessary on barren land, preventing run-off when the shit doesn't stick. It is not a metaphor meant for your mother's troubled sister.

When spoken, *cover for me* can suggests lack of ambition or follow through; whispered with masculine urgency puts others on notice to have your back regardless of their compliance.

Ketchup covered all when you didn't know better, a thick red paste pool of tomato and corn syrup serving as a mask, master concealer to the culinary challenged and underdeveloped palates.

Over time, the verb to cover was bumped by nouns *lid* and *top*, simpleton forms declaring the arrival and intersection of modern domestic preservation with cheap material commerce.

To pay it is the winnowing way of saying what lies beyond the entrance is not ordinary company; otherwise it is admission.

To take it implies what's incoming, necessary warnings for military maneuvers and mixed family functions. It is shorthand for the more insistent – *get the hell out of here.*

You prefer all the covers, in the plural as in sheets, while hoarding and hiding under cover of the night with a penchant for spoons and fetal positions.

But know this: all concealment is futile. Given time or a pinch of juicy gossip and the world will spy you uncovered, deny you and all of your coverings. In the end all covers are blown.

Theme Song for a Nondescript Gentleman

During an early evening walk along the village's cobblestone streets, a rather nondescript gentleman of forgettable appearance came to the conclusion he was being followed by the racket of two strangers.

The noise continued to follow him for some period of time, even as he made questionable turns that made no navigational sense. Eventually, he tired of the charade.

"Pardon my asking, but why are you following me?" he queried, as he turned to confront the two men behind him, one with an acoustic guitar, the other a kazoo.

"We're not following you," the guitarist sang-spoke with a Tiny Tim-like vocal. *"The music is!"*

"Well then can you make it stop?" he commanded more than questioned.

"But it's your soundtrack, your theme song," said the other with a light, saccharine-filled voice and kazoo. Dressed as a mime, his powdered face grew even paler, knowing he'd broken the covenant of his theatrical vocation in spite of his kazoo-blowing.

"You're mistaken," chortled the nondescript gentleman with an air of confidence. *"This cannot be* my *theme song."*

The heavy-set fellow with the acoustic guitar begged to differ. He continued his strumming, frequently pausing, with his face lifted to the sky while shifting to the right chord. *"Nah, this one is definitely yours."*

The nondescript gentleman could accept his labored diligence, considering the difficulty of playing while riding on one of those carnival bicycles where the front wheel is ten times the size of the one in back. But he remained wholly indifferent to his remark.

"This sounds more like Nigel's soundtrack in apartment 4E over on Livingston," the nondescript gentleman suggested.

His statement was followed with an unintelligible pantomime rebuttal, so he focused his gaze on the heavy-set fellow.

"4E? Livingston?" he continued. "Plus, I'm confident that bagpipes are in my theme song," he threw out, in hopes to throw them off their game and halt this charade of a parade through the neighborhood.

The pseudo-mime looked up at the heavy-set fellow with resignation, then whistled through his fingers and belted out the name – Charlie! – in a voice clearly unfit for a mime, his covenant clearly shot to hell at this point.

A kilt-laden lad emerged from behind a hedge of boxwoods and began running toward the commotion as his pipes flopped about his bag.

Then the nondescript gentleman, either beyond frustration or deciding to enter the game, began humming and slapping his backside as percussion, all the while moving uncomfortably closer to the pseudo-mime. It must've been the wide eyes coupled with the incessant head-bobbing and *yee-haw!* barking that, in short order, found the nondescript gentleman without his so-called theme song composers.

An elderly woman in a bathrobe caught the whole thing on video and sent it to the local television station, the channel that used to run

America's Funniest Home Videos, in hopes there was some kind of prize for her effort. It appeared on the nightly news, then the station's website and YouTube page for internet eternity. Nigel from 4E called his nondescript friend to ask what the commotion was all about. And while the whole affair made no sense to Nigel, he did comment that the music playing in the background was rather lovely, an unforgettable reminder of his tone-deaf friend whose appearance he rather fancied.

The Dawn of Spectator Sports

There are feeble-looking man-ferrets running in circles, many endless ovals. They are thin, emaciated and reeling; clearly unkempt. Onlookers get the sense they've been at this for an excruciatingly long period of time, marveling at this spectacle without definition. They are equally perplexed when a man who drops his arm next to a chalked line trampled many times over suddenly means victory.

There are huskier fellows throwing weighty parts of a forgotten pulley system around the infield, in concert with more nimble ones who invert themselves on poles and become primitive catapults reminiscent of when humans were artillery in ancient, epoch wars. Opportunities for carnage escalate with each jump, with every throw.

Then there is the man with the javelin whose activity will someday struggle to translate well to modern playgrounds. Unrefined, he calls it what it is – a spear. He looks the part: suspicious and bloodthirsty. A thrust of his weapon guarantees a win of different sorts, but he knows better. He is the penultimate gladiator, the lure and the bait, tempting a growing field of spectators whose collective interests mount with the potential of soon-to-be impaled running man-ferrets.

Make no mistake: this is what puts butts in the seats, what really gets a crowd roaring.

The Procrastinator's Story

There is the generously padded swivel chair, a notebook of half-baked ideas, a blinking cursor in its always silent and anticipatory syncopation. Add a hot cup of coffee and Mahler to the air. It is perhaps the perfect portrait of craft without production mucking things up.

This is not to say he hasn't tried. To the contrary, he has shipped off countless feeble premises into the world like sulking school children stumbling through rush-hour traffic only to meet an untimely fate.

It is reminiscent of the time he worked the line at the bureau of insects in charge of dragonflies – forming the head, thorax, rectal gills – and constantly pitching them to the wind without wings. Again, the kids, that traffic.

Thankfully he knows there are eaves that need scraped and painted, a periodical demanding he keep tabs on progress and industry. And so he goes about truncating the day, closing up shop, and giving in to the late local news and the exhaustion of being menial.

Productivity and achievement won't be measured by any formal metric, which affords him to put to rest the day's output in ample time for the night shift of hard labor to take over, where ripping hacksaws and pounding ball peen hammers resonate inside the head where the mental work of forging a perfect set of unflappable wings occur, propelling the inexplicable brilliance born of the night, just so he can hunt for it tomorrow like today's misplaced keys.

Physical Comedy

Daily, a man of portly proportions perches on the steps of the county courthouse telling jokes to passersby – think Sam Kinison without the topcoat, the screaming, or the humor. It is not just random wisecracks, but a one-man comedy routine for an intermittent audience. A series of non sequiturs about incarceration and food truck carnitas, about powdered wigs and power Whigs, about how the magistrate will see you now. He barrel-laughs at his own vague punchlines; keeps going even when nobody's approaching. For the sullen, soon-to-be fined, and exonerated, he's a poor substitute for the street preacher.

A woman of slender stature and curt attitude approaches the self-appointed court jester from behind, as if leaving the courthouse herself, barking – *"why are you doing this here? It isn't funny. You're. Not. Funny!"*

Summonsing a straight-faced response but giggling under his breath, he responds: *"These are indeed challenging times Ms. Brockovich, but the people..."*

She kicks him in the nuts; he spins and topples like a knicked bowling pin. Everyone looks toward the county sheriff sitting on the courthouse steps with his lunch-break carnitas. He silently gives her the wink and a nod instead, voids an impending assault charge.

And there it is, as if on cue – the explosion of applause like the canned hilarity of a Gary Marshall sitcom that once seemed so elusive, as he rolls uncontrollably down the courthouse steps, tumbling to a laugh track that somehow always seems a bit funnier than the scene itself.

The Sneeze ™

I didn't even want this sneeze, it being the kind that approaches like a tsunami, its quiet, rumbling tickle deep beneath the nasal septum that suddenly arrives with such potency, the first wave being one you believe you can deny and hold back, the kind of sneeze you painfully restrain with near perfection during pageants and soft-spoken eulogies, one that results in a muffled screech attempting to escape the locked orifices of one's head as the popping of your ears signals a minor victory.

Then the second wave arrives, sending a hand to the face, a face to the sleeve, with an eruption of moist annoyance and profound fear among polite company should there be a hint of a surprise lurking. Thankfully results are negative. Squinted and watery eyes momentarily subside, leading to attempts to resume conversation and good footing, only to be whacked by nature's particle mafia again, ushering in a disturbing convulsion, a full-body orgasmic lurching sans the pleasure that is so disquieting no one bothers to utter a *Gesundheit* or simple *bless you*.

I remember it vividly, it was a husky fellow in Carhartt gear outside the superstore who said – *whoa, you should patent that crazy gyration you just went through* – that got me to thinking: being ostracized to varying degrees of humiliation demands some level of protection, a badge of honor, a sign of approval that, indeed, warrants this supernatural affliction as something worth noting as special or exceptionally heinous, if solely to mitigate the knockoffs, at minimum just to earn the pandering consolation of *patent pending*, which puts me here, in the waiting room of the U.S. Patent Office as they demand greater explanation about the uniqueness of my sneeze, its commercial benefit to my applied commerce, and the proposed intellectual property connected to my irritating a-choo.

No explanation would suffice until my trademark *wheezing in threes* sneeze arrived with apocalyptic force, which, in its wild proclamation, attracted the trademark division manager, followed promptly by her cohorts from the copyright bureau, none of whom bothered to bring a clipboard or even a facial tissue, their empty gesture showing their hand and quickly realizing the opportunity has been blown.

Zen and the Art of Evel Knievel

I should have requested the sidecar instead of riding pillion, knowing my driver's tendency for the dramatic, for disaster.

I should have anticipated riding in an asphalt bobsled, assuming the car would sever from the bike itself and grind through a parking lot filled with shopping carts and doomsday spectators as helicopters clocked my record speed from above.

I should have never picked up Pirsig's classic book. I should have avoided the Phaedrus discussion altogether.

I should have avoided mentioning that there might be more in common between author and daredevil than a first name and a love of bikes.

I should have taken my mother's advice. My doctor's orders. My sanity's plea.

I should have said yes to the morphine drip.

And when Robbie wheeled a mummy-like Evel down the hospital corridor to place him in my doorway so he could chant – *next time, next time, dammit!* – it was then that I knew I should have broken my neck, too, if only to prevent me from nodding in agreement.

Small Talk with the Dead

Our friend Judy claims she can communicate telepathically with the dead. Unfamiliar with telepathy Vera and I rolled with it for years until Benito, a mutual acquaintance with a strikingly frail frame for a professional piano mover, passed away. *So ask him what it's like up there*, we prodded Judy over a cup of tea and a Danish at the neighborhood bakery. Oblivious to the commotion befitting a bakery on a Saturday morning, Judy demanded our silence. After what felt like an eternity of peering inside my porcelain cup and organizing crumbs on a saucer in outlines of western states, she quipped, *He's not up there*, without the slightest whiff of emotion. She was all purpose, flinging facts with velocity like an auctioneer proclaiming a sale. Then, more silence. I peered at Vera with a raised eyebrow. She was lip-syncing, telegraphing something my way with tightly controlled contortions that all children perform when emoting a silent plea behind a mother's back. My eyes danced at the scene – between Judy in some netherworld and Vera coming unhinged – as if I were a spectator at a hotly contested badminton match. *His headmaster has a soft spot for lilies*, Judy blurted. Headmaster? Lilies? Really? *As in Easter lilies,* I scoffed, my voice intonating the equivalent of a bell curve with a crescendo on the holiday of bodily resurrection. Vera chortled while shifting her eyes downward as if she were in search of a lifeless shuttlecock. But when Vera's eyes reconnected with mine, it was as if forfeiture was in the tarot cards, some strange truth possibly spelled out through the Danish crumbs manipulated on a saucer-as-Ouija board. Blood red carnations? Yeah, those were plausible. Black-eyed Susans? Without question. But I'll be damned if we didn't see this coming, along with a newly minted shot in the arm to Judy, albeit at Benito's expense.

House of Plates, 1872

Mathew Brady hinged together a home on a hill forged from his glass plates, his medal-less and less-than Great Exhibition. Arranging them just so, he and his beloved Juliet relived a history his government no longer wanted.

"Will you look at him, honey, always up to the task," he would say to his wife, as Lincoln, like an already risen Christ, descended the kitchen cupboards to the earth below with each new sunrise.

By midday, Mathew would lounge on his jade sofa awaiting a disheveled Whitman to pull up a seat. Juliet rocked with Clemens on the veranda, watching ironclads and sternwheelers navigate their space.

All of it predictable, right down to the harvest moon that splayed a darkened, underdeveloped Poe on the cellar doors.

Presidents, Generals, even Barnum, all marched and paraded throughout their quarters without the pains of small talk.

Then, downhill and uninvited, Juliet spied a young Georgie Eastman who had fixed his gaze upward – *"is that a stone in his hand?"* she questioned – as he vowed to shatter a window, to bring down the house. *"Ah, he's harmless."* declared the out-of-work photographer. *"What damage could he possibly do?"*

Near Death Experience

At the grave site there is a hole, a tent, a smattering of chairs, a contraption designed to lower our beloved's remains and lavish polished box into the ground, and flowers. Lots of flowers, many of which are wilting because it is an August scorcher. In the distance I see a crew of men responsible for death's logistics. The pastor's drawn-out and crawling cadence is something like death itself. Sweat is heavy on every brow. Children are near delirium. A crewman waves at me from his truck, not as in *hello* but rather in a workman-like gesture of *take your time* and I get the sense he is uninterested in the forthcoming labor as we bake in our respective gear in one-hundred-degree heat, standing outside the shade zone of a tent too small for the occasion. After every mourner has said farewell, after we dismantle the tent and toss the chairs into the truck bed, and once the casket is lowered and the contraption is carted off, I have half a mind to lie down and let those fellas dig deep and pitch cool dirt on my remains.

Things That Squawk

It is more than a little odd that two gentlemen, separately yet simultaneously, would rent the same apartment outside of Boston for some peace and quiet and productivity, learn of this quandary upon arrival, and then choose to proceed. But that's exactly how it went down. Neither knew the other, at least not formally, yet both agreed to give it a shot, to coexist in the same apartment given the great distances they both traveled for a similar purpose.

The younger fellow, who went only by Bloo, occupied a bedroom while the other, the elder gentleman, the late Mr. Edson who had been refashioned as a hologram, was fond of the apartment's public spaces and chose not to occupy tighter quarters.

Each day the co-renters would hunker down to do their work, both following their own peculiar routines accompanied by bottomless cups of stimulant, which varied depending on the time of day.

Then came a squawk from the second bedroom, the one that remained unoccupied.

In it was a crib, a blanket, a mobile of unidentifiable creatures, and a woodcut on the wall that resembled half of Edson's pre-hologram face, and the other half belonging to Bloo.

There in the middle of the floor was a blob of something, possibly humanity, but it was unclear.

It sat quietly on the bearskin rug and was covered in consonants, vowels, and small bits of punctuation. Bloo dared not to say it aloud but his snarled face gave it away, *there are no words, this blob is wholly unreadable.*

He looked at Edson's hologram. *Is this yours? Is it returnable?*

Heavens no, said Edson's hologram. *Look at me, do you think I am capable of producing that in my condition?*

Perplexed and void of maternal instincts, both men retreated to their preferred quarters and continued with their own routines meant for productivity.

When the squawking resumed, both men again met outside the doorway of the previously unoccupied bedroom that housed the handful of aforementioned peculiarities (crib, blanket, mobile, woodcut) as well as the blob of something, still quite possibly humanity, in the middle of the floor on a bearskin rug.

Bloo, who unlike Edson's hologram, had three-dimensional hands with opposable thumbs and moved to pick up and soothe the blob, even though it had grown as big and unmovable as a teenage sloth since their last visit to the once-considered unoccupied room.

The squawking blob didn't seem receptive to any sort of handling, so Bloo gave it what he had – a paperback thesaurus, the remains of his afternoon tea, and a plate of chip-chopped beef – in hopes to coax the blob back to comfort.

Edson's hologram went back to his public spaces, pacing and lamenting the wisdom of the closet-man who was never sad, and how this scenario seemed ripe with disaster, much like many of his ape poems gone awry.

He wrote in his holographic notebook while Bloo, in his bedroom, pounded away on the keys of his laptop computer.

For a long time there were no more squawks. It could've been days, months even, but neither could be sure as Edson's hologram defied the space-time continuum and Bloo was too engulfed with his work in a spartan bedroom to notice the rise and fall of light. Only the glow from his laptop computer was omnipresent.

But then Bloo felt and noticed hints of another glow, the warm orange radiance of Edson's hologram outside his bedroom door, trying not to be noticed as he listened intently, if not hoping for the slightest hint of a squawk down the hall.

Stepping away from his work, Bloo walked gingerly on his toes and met Edson's hologram in the hallway where he was leaning against a closet, where nothing was held and certainly nothing ever happened.

But something had happened in that previously unoccupied bedroom.

I think Frances is behind this, Edson's hologram said to Bloo, but it was hard to tell if it was accusation or admiration, as Edson's hologram delivered lines in a monotonous plain-speak thick with a smoker's husk.

Both men, or man and hologram to be precise, looked into the now obviously occupied bedroom where the crib had been disassembled and ignited into a small yet picturesque bonfire with some help from the thesaurus and mobile of unidentifiable creatures.

Just as Bloo made a point to save the woodcut from eminent disaster, the blob, which was no longer a blob but something resembling a Sasquatch covered in novel amounts of consonants, vowels, and punctuation – enough to now be its own stand-alone story – climbed out the window and down the fire escape to street level.

It took to foot heading southbound on Interstate 95 and began squawking for Frances in a voice that sounded surprisingly tender and nothing at all like Edson's hologram, who now had a tear in his holographic eye creating a stunning kaleidoscope of color that overtook the orange glow. Then, quite unexpected, he squawked his own beautiful, heartbreaking squawk.

Bloo gently shut his laptop, snuffing out what remained of the artificial light, believing his work here was all but finished.

Selected Poetry Titles Published by SurVision Books

Seeds of Gravity: An Anthology of Contemporary Surrealist Poetry from Ireland
Edited by Anatoly Kudryavitsky
ISBN 978-1-912963-18-8

Noelle Kocot. *Humanity*
(New Poetics: USA)
ISBN 978-1-9995903-0-7

Ciaran O'Driscoll. *The Speaking Trees*
(New Poetics: Ireland)
ISBN 978-1-9995903-1-4

Helen Ivory. *Maps of the Abandoned City*
(New Poetics: England)
ISBN 978-1-912963-04-1

John W. Sexton. *Inverted Night*
(New Poetics: Ireland)
ISBN 978-1-912963-05-8

Afric McGlinchey. *Invisible Insane*
(New Poetics: Ireland)
ISBN 978-1-9995903-3-8

Anatoly Kudryavitsky. *Stowaway*
(New Poetics: Ireland)
ISBN 978-1-9995903-2-1

Tim Murphy. *The Cacti Do Not Move*
(New Poetics: Ireland)
ISBN 978-1-912963-07-2

Clayre Benzadón. *Liminal Zenith*
(New Poetics: USA)
ISBN 978-1-912963-11-9

Thomas Townsley. *Tangent of Ardency*
(New Poetics: USA)
ISBN 978-1-912963-15-7

Matthew Geden. *Fruit*
(New Poetics: Ireland)
ISBN 978-1-912963-16-4

Marc Vincenz. *Einstein Fledermaus*
(New Poetics: USA)
ISBN 978-1-912963-20-1

Anton Yakovlev. *Chronos Dines Alone*
(Winner of James Tate Poetry Prize 2018)
ISBN 978-1-912963-01-0

Mikko Harvey & Jake Bauer. *Idaho Falls*
(Winner of James Tate Poetry Prize 2018)
ISBN 978-1-912963-02-7

Tony Bailie. *Mountain Under Heaven*
(Winner of James Tate Poetry Prize 2019)
ISBN 978-1-912963-09-6

Nicholas Alexander Hayes. *Amorphous Organics*
(Winner of James Tate Poetry Prize 2019)
ISBN 978-1-912963-10-2

John Bradley. *Spontaneous Mummification*
(Winner of James Tate Poetry Prize 2019)
ISBN 978-1-912963-13-3

John Thomas Allen. *Rolling in the Third Eye*
(Winner of James Tate Poetry Prize 2019)
ISBN 978-1-912963-15-7

Gary Glauber. *The Covalence of Equanimity*
(Winner of James Tate Poetry Prize 2019)
ISBN 978-1-912963-12-6

Charles Kell. *Pierre Mask*
(Winner of James Tate Poetry Prize 2019)
ISBN 978-1-912963-19-5

Alan Elyshevitz. *Mortal Hours*
(Winner of James Tate Poetry Prize 2020)
ISBN 978-1-912963-21-8

Henry Finch. *Reversing Falls*
(Winner of James Tate Poetry Prize 2020)
ISBN 978-1-912963-22-5

Jon Riccio. *Eye, Romanov*
(Winner of James Tate Poetry Prize 2020)
ISBN 978-1-912963-24-9

Alison Dunhill. *As Pure as Coal Dust*
(Winner of James Tate Poetry Prize 2020)
ISBN 978-1-912963-23-2

Anton G. Leitner. *Selected Poems 1981–2015*
Translated from German
ISBN 978-1-9995903-8-3

George Kalamaras. *That Moment of Wept*
ISBN 978-1-9995903-7-6

Order our books from https://survisionmagazine.com/books.htm

www.ingramcontent.com/pod-product-compliance
Lightning Source LLC
Chambersburg PA
CBHW061313040426
42444CB00010B/2620